the **Villain's** guide to

Better Living

the **Villain's** guide to

Better Living

by **neil zawacki**

illustrations by **bill brown**

CHRONICLE BOOKS
SAN FRANCISCO

Library of Congress Cataloging-in Publication Data available.
ISBN 0-8118-5666-6
Manufactured in Canada

Design by Lex MacFadden

Distributed in Canada by Raincoast Books
9050 Shaughnessy Street
Vancouver, British Columbia V6P 6E5

10 9 8 7 6 5 4 3 2 1

Chronicle Books LLC
85 Second Street
San Francisco, California 94105

www.chroniclebooks.com

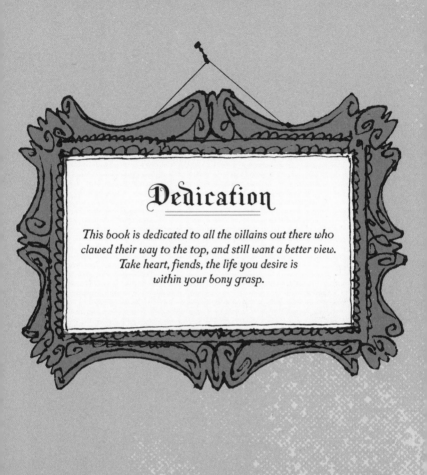

Dedication

This book is dedicated to all the villains out there who clawed their way to the top, and still want a better view. Take heart, fiends, the life you desire is within your bony grasp.

1

Introduction

*Most evil-doers lead a less than satisfactory existence,
and chances are you're one of these.*

Sure, it's good to be bad, but the life of a villain is not always about blocking out the sun. It's easy to forget about the little things that make life livable. You can conquer the world, but you can't quite conquer your checkbook. You can invent a death ray, but you still have to work nights at the video store. You can even replace all humanity with robots, but you can't convince any of them to go to the movies with you.

Most evil-doers lead a less than satisfactory existence, and chances are you're one of these. But you don't have to be. That's right—it is possible to wake up in your coffin each night and not want to destroy yourself. You can regain that gleefully evil feeling you had so long ago and thought you'd never find again.

Imagine the possibilities. You'll have more energy to tie maidens to railroad tracks. Your dastardly scheme to crash the moon into the earth will actually succeed. Your castle will be a lair for self-indulgence, and your life will be filled with minions begging to perform your every misdeed. You will be so up and so motivated that you'll want to enslave humanity again—and you'll have the strength to do it.

This will not be easy. You'll have to make some changes, and warp your worldview significantly. You'll have to shop. You'll have to clean. You'll have to mingle. But if you're ready to become an evil overlord who matters, to take the dragon by the horns and shout, "No more!" then keep reading.

Are You Satisfied with Your Evil Existence?

Perhaps you're still not convinced. If so, take this simple quiz to determine your current mood.

When you look upon your life in its current state, do you . . .

A. Destroy all nearby cities in a foaming rage?

B. Wail morosely as you claw your eyes out?

C. Smile wickedly while you wave to your adoring slaves?

When faced with a problem at work, do you . . .

A. Swat your underlings for their gross incompetence?

B. Whimper and hide in your spacecraft?

C. Overcome all odds to end up Supreme Ruler of Mankind?

You've just gotten home after a very long day and you have some free time. Do you . . .

A. Unleash your monstrous hordes on a nearby orphanage?

B. Sob uncontrollably in your dungeon for several hours?

C. Play with your moat monster? He loves you, yes he does!

How would you describe your relationship with friends and neighbors?

A. They call in nuclear strikes daily. Ha! They will fail like the last three!

B. They once hired a priest to try to banish you from this realm.

C. Great! They worship you like a god and regularly sacrifice virgins to you!

Your daily health regimen consists of the following:

A. Throwing boulders at nearby schoolchildren

B. Fleeing from villagers and angry mobs

C. Defeating entire armies without breaking a sweat

When faced with a difficult problem, do you . . .

A. Activate your doomsday device?

B. Lock yourself in a cage and hit yourself repeatedly?

C. Laugh it off? There will be other countries to conquer.

Do you smile wickedly while you wave to your adoring slaves?

If given a chance to visit anywhere on vacation, where would you go?

A. The center of a volcano, to make it erupt like your fury and destroy a vast region

B. Into the deepest parts of the ocean, never to return

C. To view the numerous statues and monuments erected in your name

How long did your last romantic relationship last?

A. Two months, until she attempted to drown you in acid

B. One week, and then she had herself committed

C. One thousand years and going strong! Immortality is such a sweet burden.

Now, add up your answers, and see what they reveal.

MOSTLY A's: You are obviously very angry in your current situation. This book is exactly what you need.

MOSTLY B's: You are apparently very depressed with your life. This book is exactly what you need.

MOSTLY C's: You are clearly deluding yourself with fake happiness. This book is exactly what you need.

When faced with a difficult problem, do you lock yourself in a cage and hit yourself repeatedly?

Do you enjoy volcanos that erupt like your own fury?

2

Home Design

Ⅹ

A villain's home is his castle. Literally. It is there that you plan your schemes, raise your dragon, and imprison the true heir to the throne. But any old bastion won't do. You need a home that reflects your dark, dead heart and suits your nefarious needs. Creating the ideal digs will require you to do things you've never done before, like work with faux finishes and shop at Bed Bath & Beyond. But if you can handle building a doomsday device, you can handle this. The following guide will help you find the suite that suits you best. Now get ready to turn your lair from drab to fabulously drab!

Gothic Vampire Vault

abode   You like a house with history in a nice, quiet neighborhood. In other words, a mausoleum. Mausoleums make excellent lairs, so stop by your favorite cemetery and appropriate one that suits your liking. It may have some other family's name on it, but you can cover that up with a nice tattered awning. Spooky mansions are a fine alternative, as long as they are crumbling with age and covered with moss and vines.

decorating   You have long hair and you're wearing a lace jabot. You're not afraid to express your poetic side, and your house shouldn't be, either. Wall-to-wall purple velvet? Yes. Numerous portraits of long-dead loves? Definitely. Huge vases full of dead flowers? Indeed. Shelves overflowing with moldering relics and mementos? Of course. Minimalism is not for you. You're an immortal, you've had plenty of time to shop, and your home reflects that. As for colors, stick to rich tones like blood red and arterial purple. Finally, don't be afraid to decorate with your own handsome likeness. The eighteenth-century portrait of yourself will look great in the dining room, and the mantel is just crying out for your marble bust. Besides, if you can't keep mirrors in the house, this is the only way you'll get a good look at yourself.

furniture   Choose heavy pieces in nice dark woods like rainforest mahogany or teak (they'll conceal mealtime blood spills). In the parlor, skip the coffee table and install a coffin table instead. You can use the space inside for storing your chapbooks and overnight guests. You'll also want a plush divan for your victims to collapse on during fainting spells, as well as some armchairs formed out of actual arm bones. A trendy minifridge is suggested for storing your blood in.

lighting Since sunlight will turn you to ash, you'll want to lose the vinyl miniblinds and cover any windows with heavy opaque curtains in damask or velvet. For ambient lighting, choose antique verdigris candelabras, gas lamps, and chandeliers to drop upon your enemies.

*Don't be afraid to decorate with your own handsome likeness.
Besides, if you can't keep mirrors in the house,
this is the only way you'll get a good look at yourself.*

quick fixes Let's face it: the vampire business has been slow for the past few years. But the bloodsucker on a budget needn't despair. It's easy to achieve high-style doom on a dime in no time flat. If you can cover up against the Sunday morning sunlight, hit the garage sales to load up on rococo accessories like carpets and candlesticks. Thrift stores are a great source for Gothic knick-nacks, picture frames, and furniture. Distress your finds further with antiquing paint and blowtoarch treatments. And be sure to pick up some old velvet curtains to use for bedspreads and uphol-stery. Finally, consider making a larcenous visit to your grandma's house. She'll never miss those old lace tablecloths, and they'll lend a nice Miss Havisham touch for next to nothing.

Mad Scientist Chalet

abode Despite touch-and-go electrical service and spotty cable reception, dark castles remain the favored home of the mad sci-entist. There's just something about gargoyles and turrets that inspires innovative brilliance. Modern brains may wish to go with a corporate lab instead.

decorating Your home must be cold, clean, lint free, and streamlined. Clutter will just get in the way when your unholy creation attempts to chase you to your death. No rugs, no art-work, no color. The only decoration you need: lots of vials and beakers connected by swirling glass tubes. Pull it all together with beeping electronic equipment that seems to serve no purpose and tremendous switches you can throw for dramatic effect.

furniture No natural materials here. Go with brushed steel and polished chrome. You'll also want a large platform to hoist up on stormy nights, and a glass table for your enormous chemistry set. It goes without saying that everything will need to be acid-proof.

The only decoration you need:
lots of vials and beakers connected by swirling glass tubes.

lighting Between the chemical explosions, the electrical pyrotechnics, the glowing frankenzombies, and the radioactive fish-headed monster-sheep, you probably won't have to worry too much about lighting. But if it's a little dim, then bottled lightning is a fine solution, as are the torches from angry villagers storming your home.

quick fixes Lacking a vendetta and a large National Science Foundation grant? Not to worry. A mad scientist's lab can still be yours, just on a smaller scale. Instead of a lab, for instance, it will probably be a converted garage. You won't have access to state-of-the-art equipment, but your nephew has a pretty nice chemistry set and an okay microscope, and he leaves his bedroom door unlocked. Robots are out of the question. But radio-controlled stuffed animals? You can have as many of those as you want.

Quick Fix: Instead of inlaid gold furniture: wicker.
Instead of mind-reading cats: non-mind-reading cats.

Egyptian Despot's Den of Curses

abode Everyone will expect you to go with a pyramid, and maybe you should. Sure, they're clichéd, but let's face it: they're really, really cool. If you just have to be different, try an underground tomb. Daring evil-doers may want to opt for a sphinx, although you'll need to be prepared for problems with local zoning laws.

decorating Stenciling isn't just for your nephew's Winnie the Pooh–themed nursery. It's also the key to an authentic-looking Egyptian den of curses. So get your stencils, your paints, and your enslaved masses ready. Start with a decorative border of scarabs and ankhs. Larger rooms will require murals. Of course, everything should be covered in hieroglyphics bearing messages of unspeakable doom. All remaining exposed surfaces should be encrusted with mosaics of turquoise, gold, beryl, and obsidian. As for accessories, mind-reading cats add a sophisticated touch, and cursed archeological treasures are a must. Beyond that, you can't go wrong with obelisks and statues of Egyptian deities. Finally, don't forget to install some secret doors and hidden chambers.

furniture Inlaid gold is really the only way to go here. It befits your royal station, and the reflection lends a lovely glow to your inbred freakish skin tone. You won't need many pieces—just a throne, an ottoman, and a few kneelers for unexpected guests. After dark, nothing says "omnipotent boy-king" or "priestess of doom" like a sarcophagus for your bed.

lighting All light should emanate from the glowing green eyeballs of your supernatural sculptures, pets, and mummified zombies. If this proves too dim, try burning torches to brighten things up. They'll also come in handy should you need to discipline the aforementioned zombies.

quick fixes   It is possible to achieve an authentic Egyptian look even without the help of a slave army. Instead of inlaid gold furniture: wicker. Instead of parquet floors: sisal rugs. Instead of mind-reading cats: non-mind-reading cats. More ambitious despots can re-create the Sahara in seconds by filling an entire room with sand. Add a potted palm, and you'll feel like you're in ancient Thebes. Finally, a curtain of wooden beads adds color and interest. A poster of *The Scorpion King* does not.

Medieval Warmongerer's Hideaway

abode   Because split-level ranches aren't big enough to house marauding hordes, most medieval warlords tend to go with a palace of some sort. This could be a fortress of doom, an obsidian citadel, or even a castle in the clouds. What's important is that it's dark and foreboding, and roomy enough for your illiterate minions. You'll also need a dungeon, a torture chamber, and, if possible, a nice screened-in patio for entertaining.

decorating   Palaces tend to be huge, so your challenge will be filling all that space. Look for big pieces that won't be dwarfed by twenty-foot ceilings. Suits of armor and iron maidens will work, as will eye-catching accessories like spiked maces. For the most part, you'll want to stick to grays and browns. Accent with a few tapestries woven with scenes of destruction—they'll lend just a touch of color and warmth. You'll also want to install a few stained-glass windows that depict your horrible rise to power, and a dungeon to house those who got in the way.

furniture   Medieval furniture sends a message: Me big strong hurty king. Comfort is not a priority. Durability is. Go with hard, chilly materials like stone and metal. If you're feeling fancy, you can encrust the surfaces with precious jewels, pearls, or artfully menacing spikes.

lighting While you could go with torches or candles, why not illuminate your palace with the fire of burning witches? You were going to dispose of them anyway, so you might as well put these heretics to good use. It's also an economical alternative to central heating. Castles are so energy inefficient.

quick fixes Think you need a time machine to get an authentic medieval look? Well, think again. If the local community theater has *Macbeth* on the calendar and a poorly guarded prop department, consider your one-stop shopping done. Load up on armor, swords, and "stone" furniture. Most likely made of Styrofoam, it will be light enough to steal even on your minions' day off.

List of Do's and Don'ts for Medieval Warmonger's Hideaway.

Post-Apocalyptic Dacha

abode   Nothing beats a bombed-out mansion or a condemned shopping mall built on toxic dumping grounds for sprawling out. In the event that the apocalypse has not happened yet, simply bulldoze a nearby establishment and move your stuff in. Try to pick someplace that houses retail establishments you favor, such as House of Pain, so you can loot the backstock.

decorating   Aim for decadent decay. Restraint and good taste have no place here. Trash fires and chemical spills do. Accessorize with old damp newspapers, cardboard boxes, and broken bottles. Geiger counters and police scanners also make great decorations, as do busted shortwave radios and smashed computers. As for artwork, stick to graffiti and vandalized billboards. Landscape with derelict *Mad Max* SUVs. Tie the whole look together with some sleeping hobos.

furniture   A trip to the dump should net you everything you need. Look for destroyed sofas, charred tables, and beds with rusty springs hanging out. If you prefer your furnishings extra-trashed, filch them from a local fraternity house.

lighting   Tires soaked in gasoline are usually the best choice, although radioactive waste makes a fine substitute.

quick fixes   This is the easiest look of all to reproduce quickly and cheaply. In fact, it's impossible to do it any other way. If the furniture you have now isn't quite ruined enough, let a feral cat and a toddler at it for half an hour or so. A teenage vandal and a can of spray paint should take care of the rest. Home, sweet home!

Restraint and good taste have no place in the post-Apocalyptic world.

Your intimidating structure will be seen across the land and make your name synonymous with terror.

Wizard's Tower of Doom

abode Maybe it's a Freudian thing, but most wizards opt for a tower. It's an excellent choice. Looming several hundred feet into the sky, your intimidating structure will be seen across the land and make your name synonymous with terror. Should towers be in short supply, the second choice, also Freudian, is a mountain cave.

decorating Your goal: scholarly sophistication. This does not mean college dorm. No *Hobbit* posters. No lava lamps. No six-way bongs. Instead, opt for walnut paneling, built-in shelves, and wall-to-wall books. Keep the color scheme muted, but not too neutral: deep reds, greens, and browns are ideal. A few plants are acceptable, as long as they have dangerous chemical properties—no ferns. Finally, a magic carpet lends a whimsical touch, and a party-sized cauldron full of bubbling margaritas says you're smart *and* fun.

furniture Shaker, Danish Modern, Louis Quatorze—the style doesn't matter. What's important is that all your furniture be under a magic animating spell. Chairs float, tables speak, beds walk. And, when they sense you're too gloomy, they all get together and cheer you up with a big musical number.

lighting Why not go with incandescent salamanders? They're portable, clean burning, renewable, and fuel efficient. Just beware the violent conflagrations that may result should you forget to feed them in a timely manner.

quick fixes The recent popularity of a certain young sorcerer is a double-edged magic sword. On the downside, it's made wizards like yourself seem less threatening. On the up, it's made wizard furnishings widely available at discount chains and drugstores. So trade your wizard hat for a baseball cap, slip on some dark glasses and a fake moustache, and head to the mall, because it's time to load up on bargain-priced cauldrons, brooms, and crystal balls. Scratch off that cursed lightning-bolt logo and nobody will know your terrible secret. Unless, of course, you fall under a truth spell.

Galactic Warlord's Cosmic Compound

abode Federal space station or an interstellar palace? The choice is yours. Just be sure it has a moon deck and those snazzy whooshing automatic doors. They really impress visitors and can be used to crush those who rise up against you.

decorating A sterile, imposing look tells alien invaders you're not to be messed with. Stick with whites and metallics, and keep the accessories to the necessary basics. Shackles are a must for keeping your captives in place. You'll definitely need lots and lots of robots, and a trapdoor leading to a gigantic alien monster, your ill-tempered pet. This comes in handy whenever any mystic warriors stop by demanding that you release their friend from carbonite. Finally, don't forget lots of mirrors, for checking out your cool Fu Manchu moustache.

furniture You can't have the dining-room chairs sliding all over the house every time you run into a meteor storm, so built-in retractable furniture is pretty much the only way to go. Warm things up with throw rugs made of space mammoth hides.

lighting Floating orbs of light are generally preferred. Laser beams are a colorful alternative, although they tend to disintegrate any passersby who walk through them. A final idea: everybody likes sconces.

quick fixes It's easy to transform your parents' basement into an out-of-this-world outer-space lounge. But covering everything with foil is a rookie move. Instead, coat the furniture in pewter-colored craft paint. Reupholster the cushions in sparkly fun fur, and cover the linoleum with a fluffy flokati rug. Mirrors and metallic mobiles lend a swanky feel. Add some futuristic lamps and a few chrome end tables, and you're cleared for takeoff.

A moon deck and those snazzy whooshing automatic doors really impress visitors.

Keeping organized will help you accomplish much more evil.

Housekeeping

cleaning your lair No one enjoys cleaning. But, like death, taxes, and the occasional nuclear accident, it's unavoidable. Even villains have to tidy up from time to time. And it's an endeavor you'll have to oversee yourself. Sure, you could entrust the chores to your evil henchmen, but they tend to steal, and they're clumsy with the good china. It's so hard to find decent help these days.

Now, we know what you're thinking: "But I like a dirty, dusty chamber of gloom. Why do I need to clean?" Well, for starters, because it's where you eat and sleep, and you need to maintain a certain level of hygiene. A little grime is fine—preferable, even—but there's a limit. Sure, it helps if during a visit your enemy gets infected with flesh-eating bacteria, but not if you do. Furthermore, keeping organized will help you accomplish much more evil. You can hardly take over the world when your disintegration ray is hidden under a year's worth of pizza boxes and Mountain Dew cans.

You'll therefore want to clean your lair at regular intervals (say, every other week, or once a millennium). Start by dealing with the big things: trash fires, cauldron spills, and dragon accidents. To remove any unsightly stains simply consult the sidebar on page 35. You may also want to think about Scotchgarding your lair. For scorch marks and acid holes, board up the room and never look back.

Next you'll tackle the clutter. While you may be proud of your many weapons and collector plates, leaving them scattered about is distasteful. You need to find a place to store them, such as a closet, bedroom, or orbiting space station. If there's still not enough space, just get rid of them by tossing them in a bottomless pit or volcano. You do need room for your new mad experiments, after all.

Acid spills have ruined many a fetching frock.

Some Common Stains and Ways to Get Them Out

blood   This is fairly easy—just soak the item in cold water and apply spot remover. If that doesn't work, consider changing your color scheme to red.

acid   You won't be able to do much about the holes, but the black marks can be fixed with a little bleach and free time.

holy water   Be careful here. Stand back and instruct an underling to treat the stain with copious amounts of vinegar. He'll die a horrible death, but at least the holy water will be removed.

slime   You'll be relieved to learn that most sewage-based stains can be treated with rubbing alcohol and a clean cloth. Entrails are more difficult, and steel-wool pads may be needed to remove baked-on, caked-on goo.

black hair dye   Sorry, but this stuff never comes out. That's what you get for deciding to be the slickest villain of them all.

Home Security

protecting your home   Home security is very important, even to bad guys like yourself. There are all sorts of nefarious folk out there—salesmen, census workers, Girl Scouts—who want nothing but to do you ill. You will therefore want to employ the best security system possible, not just to protect your family (what have they ever done for you?) but to safeguard your piles and piles of wealth. Sweet, sweet gold. Gold never hurts your feelings.

The classic villain security system is a moat/spiked fence combo. The moat can be occupied by a ravenous tentacle monster, while the fence provides nearly impenetrable security. For added protection, consider a wall of brambles. It's fairly easy to maintain, and the pricklies really do hurt.

If hardware's not your thing, you may want to consider magic. A spell can make your home invisible to the naked eye, or it can prompt fireworks to shoot off whenever anyone gets too close. A charm that induces slumber in visitors is another favorite, as it both prevents entrance and provides you with tasty people-snacks for your dragon. Forgetfulness charms are another excellent option, making intruders forget why they came in the first place. Spend your money on home protection—you'll be glad you did.

The classic villain security system is a moat/spiked fence combo.

Evil-doers can take a piece of nature and corrupt it to their liking.

Gardening

Villains aren't big outdoors people. They'll put a lot of energy into the lair, but very little into the lawn. That's a shame. Your backyard is a great untapped resource. While most villains use theirs for storing their doomsday devices, consider transforming yours into a garden of doom. Nature is not the exclusive dominion of singing waifs and their bluebird companions. Evil-doers can take a piece of it too, and corrupt it to their liking. You simply have to decide what kind of garden you want.

the poisonous garden   One of the most popular options is the poisonous garden. Containing hemlock, nightshade, and the longtime favorite, belladonna, this sinister selection of plants will serve all your villainous needs. Simply grow them in your backyard and give them proper care, and you will gain a near-endless source of lethal toxins. Excellent for when you want to poison the princess or add a deadly edge to your blade, or simply make teatime more interesting.

the carnivorous garden   Another superb choice is a carnivorous garden of hungry meat eaters. You can fill your backyard with enormous Venus flytraps, Amazonian pitcher plants, and exotic shrubberies from outer space. These ravenous flora subsist entirely on flesh and are sure to bring a country feel, and plenty of entertainment, to your Gothic lair. This garden also has the added benefit of home security—any heroes or thieves who trespass late at night stand an excellent chance of being eaten.

the endless hedge maze   Evil-doers who do not wish to maintain a traditional garden may want to consider an endless hedge maze instead. These living labyrinths can be crammed with all manner of deadly booby traps and lethal insects. Through simple space-warping technology they can be made endless, with vegetative passages that mislead visitors and circle back on themselves. Truly fiendish, and a great source of entertainment for your guests—and for you.

Pest Control

Pests and vermin are an unfortunate nuisance plaguing every estate. It might be pixies in the attic, gnomes in the garden, or mermaids in the bathtub. You might even encounter helpful house spirits, bearing offers of good luck in exchange for kind words and lodging. Your response to these freeloaders should always be the same: chase the fiends out and send them packing.

For the most part a broom should do the job. Simply sweep up the spritely varmints and chuck them out a window. Should you wish to dump them with a more permanent method, however, you will need to purchase some fairy poison. Brewer's yeast is particularly effective. Fairies can't handle its healthy, foul-tasting effects. Just sprinkle it over favorite fairy foods like candied violets and caramels, and you'll wake up fairy-free.

If this tactic fails, you may have to resort to more drastic measures. You can hire an exterminator—expensive, but worth it for his or her fairy-trapping skills. Fumigation is another option, although it can be annoying, not to mention embarrassing, to have one's castle draped in a striped tent. Know that in the end it will be worth it, because coming home to a lair without shoe-repairing elves is a most wonderful thing indeed.

Simply sweep up the spritely varmints and chuck them out a window.

41

Home Improvement

fixing up that dungeon Have your fellow villains got you down? Are they making fun of you because your once dank and gloomy dungeon now has a hole in the ceiling, allowing fresh sunlight to beam through? Fret not, my fiend. With just one afternoon of work you can have your dungeon fixed up as dismally as in the olden days!

The prison should be your primary area of focus. Check to make sure nobody has escaped, and give the locks and bars a good cleaning. Make sure the doors are properly creaky, and attach a ball and chain to any captive who has grown too unruly. Decorate with a few dangling skeletons, and your prisoners will soon be oohing and aahing over their ghastly new cells!

The torture chamber should be next on your list, though it may be the most difficult restore. Frequency of use means wear and tear, so you may have to break down and purchase a new cat-o'-nine-tails. Most iron maidens can be repaired with some iron spikes, however, and motor oil works wonders for dirtying up your thumbscrews. Your rack, sadly enough, is probably on its last legs, so just throw it out and get a new one.

See? That wasn't so hard, and what a difference a day makes! You can now show off your dungeon without shame. Why not reward yourself with a nice glass of pickled fairy juice? You've earned it.

Decorate with a few dangling skeletons, and your prisoners will soon be oohing and aahing over their ghastly new cells!

3

Health

—◆———☠———◆—

Conquering the known universe takes a lot out of a person, so it's time to focus on a matter that should be of great importance to you—your health. You may roll your three eyes at this, confident in your ability to pick up tractors and launch them at your enemies, but this superior prowess will not last forever. You need to maintain your intimidating physique, watch what you eat, and be prepared for horrible diseases. Think about it: If you haven't got your health, you haven't got anything (except an army of minions, a castle, and piles of gold).

Nutrition and Lifestyle

obtaining that sickly glow One of the surest signs that a villain is in proper health is a sickly glow. Pallid skin, prematurely white hair, profuse sweating . . . these mean you are doing something right. But how to attain such a dismal state? There are several ways.

Though not recommended, you can go the cosmetic route. Makeup, hair dye, and a water spritzer all work wonders toward achieving the "near dead" look. But it is not just a look we're talking about here—it's your actual health, metabolism, and eating habits. You will need to pay attention to your lifestyle itself if you are serious about coming off like an ailing wreck.

So what should you do? How about spending an hour each day bathing in pond muck? Or ravaging your body through dark magic? You can also subject yourself to horrible experiments that require you to inject yourself regularly with poisonous serums and toxins. Watching C-SPAN for any period of time will invoke a similar effect.

By performing these simple acts, your body should begin to shrivel and you will gain that wonderful sickly pallor. Cats (other than yours) will hiss, townspeople will flee, and you'll be secure in the knowledge that you'll be around to menace the world for years to come.

eating right Evil-doers are notorious for their poor eating habits. They'll start tinkering with their rocket turrets, get too busy to cook a real meal, and subsist on junk food, flies, and empty calories instead. This inevitably results in low energy. If you want to become the greatest criminal mastermind possible, it's time to put down that Twinkie and start eating right.

You can achieve this through some simple changes in your diet. Stop eating any fruits and vegetables, as they will cause nothing but problems. Try the souls of the damned. Low in cholesterol and high in fiber, they are appetizer, meal, and just desserts all in one.

Blood is another highly nutritious food, and it has the added benefit of putting a spring in your step. Listen to those vampires—they know what they're talking about. Bitter tears are good for electrolytes, although they're somewhat hard to obtain. You will need to spin tales of horrible sorrow to your subjects, and then lap up their tears while they're sobbing. Failing that, rent *Beaches*.

Obtaining that sickly glow.

Life-Threatening Illness

dealing with heart problems It is a sad fact of life that, as they age, many villains begin to develop heart problems. We speak not of the traditional mortal perils of heart disease and angina, although those can be concerns as well. No, we instead refer to that terrible lingering force called love.

It can strike without warning. An ordinary evil-doer, with a heart two sizes too small, will wake one Christmas morning and suddenly regain the accursed ability to feel again. Don't let that happen to you! Take preemptive measures! Too many villains have fallen from great heights, so we suggest that you enact a simple procedure to immunize yourself: Bury your heart in a jar underground.

Any container will do, but we suggest one that can withstand the test of time and degrading effects of the environment. It won't serve you well if your jar cracks a hundred years down the road and all manner of muck gets in. You may also want to place a charm inside to ward off holy prayers and spells as well as the ever-present problem of mold spores.

As for removing your heart, it should be fairly easy provided you have lost all ability to feel and care. Simply apply a mild anesthetic and pluck your heart from your chest, placing it gently in the container of your choosing. You'll then want to bury it six feet deep, along with a few decoy hearts. Mission accomplished, and a potential health crisis averted.

Take preemptive measures: Bury your heart in a jar underground.

An extra eye or tentacle is always helpful.

Which Disease Is Right for You?

Sometimes being healthy is not a villain's best option. And while it's true that disease has its downside—those embarrassing open-backed hospital gowns don't look good on anyone—it also has its advantages. Sickness can do wonders for your skin, producing enchanting rashes and growths you'd never otherwise enjoy. It can make you meaner than you've ever hoped to be. Diseases can be your friend, so why not embrace one? Your evil nature should make you immune to their lethal properties, and the side effects will provide you with numerous delights. Some of the more popular choices:

tomb rot   Favored by necromancers and mummies alike, tomb rot is the ailment for evil-doers who don't like visitors. Should some foolish archeologists come knocking on your tomb, simply afflict them and watch them wither before your eyes!

mutations   Though they are not a disease per se, you may want to cultivate some mutations anyway. An extra eye or tentacle is always helpful, as is the ability to shoot spikes on command. To attain such aberrations, simply go down to your local toxic waste dump and roll around a bit.

Disease As a Weapon

the plague   This spectacular disease managed to slay a third of Europe. Known for its high death rate and oozing pustules, the plague is smelly and fast-acting. Just think of the joys of having it at your command!

spontaneous human combustion   Previously considered a tragic phenomenon, spontaneous human combustion is now a villain's delight. By gaining control over its fiery effects you can singe bystanders and toast a perfect marshmallow at the same time.

rabies   Villains who contract this delightful disease will suffer from uncontrollable rage and clouded judgment. Even better, anyone you bite will start foaming at the mouth within three days time! There will be no choice but to put them down like Old Yeller, provided they don't get their own talk radio show first.

chicken pox   This childhood ailment is a villain's dream come true. Besides vastly improving your appearance, it's highly infectious and will cause any heroes you touch to break out in unsightly red spots. They will be forced to stop what they're doing and spend the day in bed, leaving you free to rob banks with impunity.

Spontaneous human combustion: By gaining control over its fiery effects, you can singe bystanders and toast a perfect marshmallow at the same time.

*You need to begin an exercise program or else be
smashed like a bug underfoot.*

Other Health Tips

exercise those old bones Have you noticed a change in your physical appearance lately, with your once-rippling muscles being replaced with a beer gut and love handles? Don't weep, for such things are common in villains age two hundred and older. The dark power starts to wane, and you need to begin an exercise program or else be smashed like a bug underfoot.

As a rule, you'll want to devote at least an hour each day to exercise. Use your time-halting powers to ensure that you will not be interrupted. Start with calisthenics, stretching your arms and tentacles until they are warmed up properly. You can also engage in a number of evil aerobics programs such as Jazzercise or Richard Simmons', provided you are brave enough. Up-tempo music like funeral dirges can make this more fun. Remember to keep your heart rate up for at least thirty minutes!

Next, it's time for your main workout. You want to build up muscle, so lift heavy objects like your robot or a nearby ball and chain. Be sure to have one of your henchmen spot you, lest tragedy occur. If your self-discipline fails, remember that bodybuilding can ultimately pave your way to world domination.

Physical endurance should be next on your list, so spend ample time performing pull-ups, doing sit-ups, and pushing a boulder up a hill in Hades for all eternity. You'll want to devote your remaining time to running—always good for the villainous heart. Best of all, it's easy to incorporate into your daily routine. You have to chase wounded foes and flee from the heroes, anyway—why not push yourself an extra lap?

Soon, your health will improve and those hateful love handles will disappear. You'll look great in your tuxedo at the evil high-school reunion.

Alternative Medicine

When traditional medicine fails, it's time to consider drastic means. While they may seem odd to you, with their lack of dark prayers and newts' eyes, modern medicine and investment in pharmaceuticals can do wonders. Keep an open mind, if you can.

antibiotics Designed to kill infections, antibiotics are tiny pills that will prevent you from getting sick. Side effects include diarrhea, vomiting, and difficulty swallowing.

painkillers While it may seem inconceivable for you to avoid or stop pain, there are powerful drugs you can take that will enhance your performance. Just shop around; you'll find plenty of doctors willing to whip out a prescription.

antidepressants Want to turn that frown upside-down? Try drowning yourself in antidepressants! You'll find these mood-altering drugs are just what the doctor ordered to maintain that perfect level of psychotic rage.

surgery Medical problems not involving decapitation can often be fixed via surgery. They'll knock you out and cut you open. It will be just like the date you had last Thursday!

If nothing seems to work and you're fading fast, then you can always just clone yourself.

Finding a Therapist

Mental health should be a substantial concern for you. While many evil-doers embrace the concept of madness, it can be quite distracting when your attempts at global domination are constantly hamstrung by father issues or the need to flip a light switch a certain number of times. In these cases it is suggested you seek out a therapist to help you get your head back on straight.

There are a wide variety to choose from, including Freudian, Jungian, and the kind that hit you repeatedly with a stick. They're all in the Yellow Pages, so let your bony fingers do the walking. These trained professionals will listen politely as you describe your many woes, as well as pump you so full of drugs that your Mr. Hyde personality surfaces slightly less.

One of the most effective techniques they have at their disposal is the ever-popular word association. It reveals a lot when the word "childhood" makes you think of "nightmare," or "horrible failure" is followed by "me." The subsequent disposing of your therapist to keep your terrible secret will further expose a great deal about your character.

Electroshock therapy is another great way to cure your raging psychosis. This time honored technique has long been used to calm the beast within, all through the simple application of 10,000 volts to the cerebral cortex. It also occasionally grants bizarre electro-powers, so be sure the dial is set to full.

If all else fails, you should consider getting a lobotomy. Sure, it'll diminish your mental faculties by 95 percent, but so will reality television, music videos, and running for congress. At least with the lobotomy your stress levels will be relieved, and give you something in common with the rest of the drooling masses.

Immortality

Perhaps you think a health regime sounds like too much work. So many diseases to catch, so many crunches and squats—it's a lot to take on. Should you decide it's not for you, perhaps you should eschew your health entirely and go for immortality. It's a tricky business, but one that will ultimately solve all your problems.

Dark magic is probably your best bet. There are ancient necromantic rituals that will transform you into one of the undead, usually a vampire or mummy. The only drawback is that these techniques tend to backfire and destroy half the countryside should you mix in the wrong number of salamander tongues. Flame-retardant suits are thus recommended should you go this route.

Mad science is another possibility. It's surprising how often getting struck by 10,000 volts will render a person immortal. Glowing green elixirs have a similar effect, as do bombardments of lethal radiation. You should be prepared for the occasional side effect, however, like growing fifty feet tall and attacking Tokyo. Since that was probably on your itinerary anyway, it shouldn't be too much of a problem.

Pacts with supernatural forces are a final and excellent choice. You don't really have much use for that soul anyway, so why not trade it for eternal youth? Just remember to read the contract in full ahead of time, because the Devil loves ironic twists. You won't be very happy if you become a wax mannequin upon signing, so have your lawyers check for any loopholes.

You should be prepared for the occasional side effect,
like growing fifty feet tall and attacking Tokyo.

4

Work

✠

Evil-doers have long been a part of the business world. They work as CEOs, corporate lobbyists, lawyers, accountants, and even video store clerks. To every job they bring malice and a desire to crush their enemies underfoot. It's truly a wonderful thing to be in a position of power, and by entering the nine-to-five grind you can begin your glorious ascent to the top.

The Grind

job interviews Before you can become part of the working world, you have to get an actual job interview. This is a somewhat difficult and mentally exhausting experience, but it will be worth it when you receive that first paycheck. You simply need to follow a set of basic rules, and use your 300 IQ and snakelike tongue to the best of your ability.

Start by putting your resume together. You want to emphasize your achievements, so describe any galaxies you've conquered in extremely large font. Your accomplishments don't need to be in chronological order, so if you killed Superman five years ago, put that up top. Education should appear near the end, listing your university degrees (go ahead and fib) and any special certification you might possess in areas like sorcery, martial arts, or cake decorating.

Next, you'll go after that interview. Search the classifieds for help-wanted ads. Respond to any postings for the job of "despot," "varlet," or anything else that sounds fun (but be warned: "corporate headhunter" is not at all what it sounds like). If that fails to net a reply, cold-call corporations that sound especially evil to ask if they have any openings.

Eventually you should get an interview, to which you will want to wear your best suit. You might think you look better in full battle armor, but go for the conservative look here: cape, ascot, top hat, and pointy boots. Greet your interviewer with the appropriate pleasantries, and then prepare to lie horribly.

Be commanding as you speak, and don't be afraid to play up your strengths. If you have the ability to possess people or design matter-transmuters, let them know. If you don't, tell them you do. Modesty and honesty will get you nowhere but the welfare line. So give it all you've got, and you'll soon be on the fast track to villainous success.

Go for a conservative look for the interview: cape, ascot, top hat, and pointy boots.

resume builders When designing your resume, you may have trouble making it sound just right. Though they use the same villainous tactics, the corporate world occasionally uses different language. This is all for public relations, of course. Some examples:

Experience	Becomes
Planning a bank heist	Project management skills
Inventing a weather machine	History of creating an adaptable environment
Raising an army of the dead	Knowledgeable in training coworkers
Destroying the world	Highly skilled in downsizing
Escaping from jail	Ability to dispense with unwanted situations
Blocking out the sun	Deflected illumination on company practices
Reading the *Necronomicon*	Up-to-date on all current literature
Poisoning the king	Assisted in transition of former management
Selling your soul	Strong financial sense

Top Ten Interview Questions and How to Respond

I. Why do you want to work here? Be honest: Tell them "money, power, and the chance to crush my enemies." They'll like that.

II. What do you know about our company? You'll have to do some research here, but be sure to mention any hostile takeovers or pending environmental lawsuits.

III. What are your strengths? You undoubtedly have several, so start with your genius, move on to your physical prowess, and end with your ability to make people's heads explode.

IV. What are your weaknesses? "I'm a workaholic" is always a safe response. Make sure you don't mention your fatal flaw, be it the holy cross or Rice Krispies. They'll just use it against you later.

V. What do you think you could bring to this job? Sometimes clichés don't work. Rather than saying, "Solid work ethics and a willingness to get a job done!" try "Death, destruction, and lots of pointy weapons."

VI. Do you work well with others? A proper response would be "As long as they are my mindless, terrified slaves." It shows a working knowledge of the corporate world.

VII. How do you keep yourself motivated? Tell the interviewer about your thirst for power and strong desire for revenge, and they'll soon be nodding along with you.

VIII. How do you respond to tough situations? Don't hesitate to admit that you use acid, knockout gas, or whatever tactics are necessary.

IX. Where do you see yourself in five years? While you may be tempted to say, "Standing over your weeping, chained body," try to be more moderate: "Standing over everyone but your weeping, chained body."

X. Why are the police arresting you right now? Assure your interviewer that they have the wrong man, and you couldn't have possibly robbed those five banks as they claim.

dealing with the commute Each workday for a villain tends to be the same. You leave your lair with briefcase in hand, kiss your Witch Queen on the cheek, and head off to work. Forty minutes later and you're still not there, because you're stuck on the interstate! Traffic. It's an evil-doer's worst enemy, especially when you've got a ten o'clock meeting with the Dark Lord.

You will therefore want to join a carpool, if possible. There are always other warlords and sorcerers who need to get to their job at the photo mart, so why not band together? The four of you can zip past traffic to your destination, laughing at the other commuters along the way. Just be prepared for the occasional personality conflict, since people who've conquered nearby kingdoms tend not to compromise on matters like choosing a radio station.

Those who cannot find villains to ride with will have to travel solo. Your drive will be much longer, although some entertainment can still be had. Rush-hour traffic is an excellent place to unleash your swarm of monkey men, and casting fireballs has been known to improve gridlock. By using these techniques, you'll at least have a smile on your face when you reach your job, and you'll be ready to mop those floors with vigor.

There are always other warlords and sorcerers who need to get to their job at the photo mart, so why not band together?

surviving coworkers The work environment can be extremely taxing for many villains. It's not just the work and the deadlines; it's the morons you have to deal with every day. Coworkers can drive an evil-doer crazy. So how to deal with these terrible twits?

One way is to obtain a time machine to go back to the past and ensure they are never born. But be careful not to tinker with anything else, or you may sentence us all to a future without doughnuts or digital cable.

There are some coworkers you just can't get rid of, however. They are either too valuable to the company or they possess a talent for limited invulnerability, like spin doctors and damage-control experts. This doesn't mean you have to learn to live with them—you simply have to be sneakier. Drop shrinking potions into their coffee mug and smear fast-acting cement on their phone receiver. It won't really change anything, but you'll feel a lot better inside.

making the workday go faster Most villains discover that working a day job is not particularly taxing. It can be downright monotonous at times, with your superior intellect wasted on such questions as, "Would you like fries with that?" What you need are ways to make time go faster, and preserve your dwindling sanity. Suggestions include . . .

- Construct chain-mail suits out of paper clips.

- Undermine your coworkers' self-confidence with passive-aggressive comments about their weight.

- Play a live-action version of minesweeper.

- Install a self-replicating Artificial Intelligence on the office network that wants to destroy humanity.

- Cast hexes on every third person to come through your door.

- Replace your boss's brains with Folger's crystals and see if he can tell the difference.

- Spin around in your chair until you get really dizzy.

- Design doomsday devices on the office memo pad.

- Spread the seeds of discontent that will ultimately lead to the company's downfall.

These simple tricks should make the day fly by and put you in the right mindset for your night job as Conqueror of All Humanity.

how to get a raise With the cost of living as high as it is in today's evil world, it's no wonder so many villains are going broke. They just don't have enough money to pay for their floating citadels and orbiting doom rays. You'll consequently want to improve your cash flow as much as possible and attempt to get a raise at your job.

Toadying is the best way to achieve this. Find a superior to attach yourself to, and perform her every whim no matter how degrading. Cajole her with constant flattery and be a yes-man, even when her projects are doomed to failure. She will soon appreciate your sniveling patheticness and toss gold coins your way like scraps to a dog at dinnertime.

Villains with a modicum of self-respect may actually have to work to achieve a raise. You will need to produce results so amazing that even the boys upstairs will notice your brilliance but won't be so intimidated that they consider you a threat. Foreclose on petting zoos and destroy small countries' water sources with gusto, but always leave some room for improvement. Compensation should eventually come your way.

If it does not, you may need to resort to backstabbing and blackmail. Your boss surely has horrible secrets he does not want the world to know, so root out those early photos of him on the pep squad. He'll undoubtedly buckle and give you a raise, and perhaps a corner office as a well. If not, just kidnap him and take his.

*Find a superior to attach yourself to, and perform her
every whim no matter how degrading.*

A union is a wickedly powerful force,
and one you should consider joining.

joining a union Once you've been at your job for a while you may notice something odd—large groups of people meeting in dark chambers and discussing sinister ways to influence policy. No, not the secret society down in 3C—we're talking about your labor union! It's a wickedly powerful force, and one you should consider joining.

There are numerous benefits. You will gain access to an army of disgruntled workers who can bring management to its knees. You will learn ruthless backstabbing and subterfuge techniques, as well as develop lifelong relationships with organized crime. Plus, you'll get to find out where Jimmy Hoffa is buried.

All is not sunshine and roses, however. Drawbacks include widespread bureaucracy and the occasional enslavement of a family member. There are also outrageous dues that would be better spent improving your lair. You'll just have to weigh the positive with the negative and decide if it's worth it. Are you a solitary evil-doer, or do you prefer unruly mobs?

unemployment for villains The state of the current economy is such that employment is no longer a guarantee. Even though you may have a degree in Ultimate Evil, with five years of experience in looting and pillaging, it is not uncommon to come back from lunch these days and see a pink slip waiting at your desk.

Welcome to the world of unemployment, where you spend one hour a day looking for work, and the rest sitting on your couch watching the Home Shopping Network. It's a sad state of affairs for someone who once successfully devoured the sun, but one you can still take advantage of.

Welcome to the world of unemployment.

The main way to do so is to register for unemployment. Don't feel ashamed. Other masterminds have done so and it's gotten them through the hard times. You just need to convince your caseworker that you have searched for employment (mind control rays are suggested), and, once you do, you'll have enough to pay the rent on your lair till the end of the month. No sweat.

Your problem then becomes one of finding activities to fill your sudden glut of free time. Motivated evil-doers can spend it performing such tasks as digging a bottomless pit, but most just end up wandering their castle in their bathrobe. Don't despair if this happens to you, because another job will eventually be yours, and you'll once again be running a criminal empire with the best of them.

White Collar Crime

If you are successful in your chosen career path, you'll eventually break through the glass ceiling and become the Corporate Bastard you've always dreamed of being. The rules are a little different for the all-powerful, however. You'll need a business strategy, methods for eliminating waste, and proven ways to transform your workers into a docile slave force.

business tips and corporate "ethics"

These days it is quite in vogue for an enterprise to have a code of conduct. Yours should be no exception. Follow these simple dictums, and you'll be running a Fortune 500 company in no time!

- Leadership demands ruthlessness, contempt, and thick boots for grinding people underfoot.

- Teamwork requires sacrifice, often to the Dark Gods.

- Deliver what is expected and nothing more, unless it's a knife in the back.

- Provide low-quality products that attack customers while they sleep.

- Do unto others before they do unto you.

- Do damage control unto others before they sue you.

- Promote strife and discord at all turns—it's good for business.

- Bribery is, of course, at all times acceptable.

- The Golden Rule: Those who have the gold, rule.

*You'll eventually break through the glass ceiling and become
the Corporate Bastard you've always dreamed of being.*

Do not put much thought into whom you are firing.

downsizing Members of upper management often have to take drastic steps in order to keep the business afloat. Deadwood and longtime workers nearing pension time have to be cast off in order for the corporation to thrive, and downsizing is the way to go. It's a cost-saving measure that's both utterly heartless and maliciously fun.

Do not put much thought into whom you are firing. You can just tack the company roster on a dartboard and throw with abandon. Once you've got ten or twenty names, call them into your office and let them know that little Timmy won't be getting his braces. They'll beg and plead pathetically, and you can make a rousing game of it. When you finally get tired, send them on their way with a warning not to let the door hit them on the way out.

There are a few repercussions to downsizing, however. Since your company will now be smaller, you will have less of a food source to draw upon. This is not necessarily a bad thing, considering you could stand to lose a few pounds. They lose their jobs, you lose the flab—in the end, it's win-win.

motivating your minions Evil-doers who manage to claw their way into management positions often discover their job is more difficult than previously imagined. Your minions won't do what you tell them to do, and you hear them doing impressions of you when you leave the room. They're just too lazy, too complacent, too unaware that you can recycle them as fire lighters. They have to be motivated. Fortunately, there are many wonderful ways to do this, applying positive *or* negative reinforcement:

- Whippings
- Bribery
- Lots and lots of shouting
- Ogre supervisors
- Free trips to the first circle of hell
- Solitary confinement in the supply closet
- A shiny gold star for whoever does best

Your underlings should soon become a helpful slave force. Congratulations on becoming a true middle manager!

There are many wonderful ways to motivate your minions.

5

Social Life

Making fiends is easy. But making friends—that's another story. It can be so hard to show your softer side, to smile without baring your fangs. And yet you must. No villain is an island, not even in this increasingly solitary world. You need allies, people to assist you in the darkest of hours. It may seem strange that villains require friends and significant others, but it's the truth—who else will help you conquer the known world and subjugate the weak?

Forging Alliances

creating life One way to make friends is the wholly absorbing act of creating life. Whether in a mad scientist's laboratory or high school chemistry classroom, this activity is guaranteed to bring new people into your life. And, if you have no family, it's a great opportunity to make one.

To start off, you'll need to obtain some body parts. The local cemetery is an excellent source for these, and you'll likely want to mix and match as you search for the best arms, legs, torso, and brain for your creation. Sew it all together with needle and thread, and be sure to attach bolts on the sides of the neck.

You'll now have to bring it to life. Electricity is your best bet, so hoist your creation up on a metal platform the next time a lightning storm rages. If you're impatient, just use some tesla coils or the jumper cables from your car. The heart of your artificial human should soon begin to beat, and you'll have a friend to last the ages.

Please keep in mind that your patchwork monster will likely feel alone in this vast, uncaring universe. It is thus suggested that you build a bride for him. Undead monsters generally prefer shrieky, inarticulate ladies with bad perms. Together the three of you can sit around the dinner table like the best of friends, at least until the torch-bearing villagers arrive.

Creating life is guaranteed to bring new people into your life.

Secret societies.

other ways to make friends One way to forge alliances is by offering assistance. Do you wish you could horn in on the clique that needs a fifth Horseman of the Apocalypse? Have they locked their keys in the car? Come to their aid, and it'll be a favor not soon forgotten.

When it's your turn to need a hand, be sure to call in all the favors your new friends owe you. A friendship means nothing if you don't exploit it, so be sure to recruit your pals when your temple of doom is raided by holy knights. And maybe, just maybe, your buddies won't try to snatch up your empire for themselves.

where to meet them:

secret societies These ancient societies have existed for thousands of years and secretly control all the world's governments. This is really true! An excellent place to network and find someone to accompany you to the hockey game.

Seedy space bars.

thieves' underground   The gathering place for all who break the law or just like to be bad. You can fence stolen objects here, buy a new set of lock picks or an election, and make all sorts of friends who will try to stab you when you're not looking.

seedy space bars   Nowhere else will you find a more wretched hive of scum and villainy. Alien bounty hunters, space pirates, and Martian thugs all gather together here, looking for a fight and a new drinking companion.

demonic cults   There are numerous occult circles filled with those who want nothing more than to summon demons and bring about the destruction of mankind. These are kindred spirits who should invite you into the fold immediately.

the gym   Watch out on this one. This is a gathering spot for villains, to be sure, but they are especially nefarious types like personal trainers. Venture with caution, and keep your hand on your wallet at all times.

Mind Control

Sometimes kind words and flattery just aren't enough. No matter how much you cajole and plead, that evil mastermind won't agree to be your friend. In these cases it is important to resort to more drastic methods.

Hypnotism is a superb tool for control freaks. Utilized by such evil-doers as Rasputin, this method can make even the most iron-willed person cluck like a chicken. You simply need a pocket watch and spiraling eyes, and Anastasia will be your slave by lunchtime.

Villains with supernatural powers can use them to cloud the minds of men, turning foes into friends. Vampires are excellent at entrancing the weak, demons possess a brilliant knack for corruption, and pod people just have a way of making you see things their way. If you've got an unholy gift, run with it!

Technological wizardry is your other option, and the best choice for those not living in a fantasy world. All you have to do is invent or purchase an orbital mind-control laser, and that alliance you so desperately need will be yours. Friendship can't be forced, people say, but those people are horribly, horribly wrong.

Hypnotism: you simply need a pocket watch and spiraling eyes.

*Call your friend up on the phone (or scrying pool) and
let him know you're free for a few hours.*

How to "Hang Out"

Now that you've got friends, you need to spend some time in their actual presence. This may seem odd, considering you already have their oath of fealty, but "hanging out" cements relationships and can even be somewhat fun. You may be confused by the social mores, however, so just do the following:

Call your friend up on the phone (or scrying pool) and let him know you're free for a few hours. Hint that failure to meet will result in unbridled destruction. Disconnect the call, and then pop in the shower to get rid of the smell of chemical fires. Dress casually, and don't forget to bring along a chest of ill-gotten gold for some spending money.

When you arrive at your pal's place, greet him in a positive manner. At no point should you attack or behead him—that's for enemies, and this guy's your friend. Ask him about his day, and feign interest in everything he says.

When the topic of conversation switches to you, hold forth on your many achievements and allow him to praise you sufficiently. Accept any offerings or graven images, and once an appropriate amount of time has passed, depart. If he has done well, let him know that he has performed his role admirably, and that you will give him a favorable reference in the future.

Good Pets for Villains

Evil-doers who are unable to make any friends may want to seek out animal companionship. Pets will stay with you when humans will not, miffed over some supposed gaffe like spilling acid on the rug or exiling them from the kingdom. Head to your local pet shop and pick out a new friend, with possibilities including . . .

dragon A true classic, dragons are the ideal pet for villains who have large piles of gold that need guarding. Simply feed them the occasional princess and rub their belly nightly, and you'll have a friend that will last the ages.

fluffy white cat The favored pet of criminal masterminds around the world. Revealing your master plan just isn't the same without holding one of these fancy felines in your arms.

moat monster Notable for their many tentacles, moat monsters are practical only if you have a large body of water to keep them in. Bathtubs will suffice, but this tends to make using the bathroom a bit difficult.

one-eyed alien Believe it or not, a crashed UFO can sometimes mean a new friend. One-eyed aliens make excellent pets for those who don't mind the language barrier and high long-distance bills.

hellhound Man's best friend, provided the man is an unholy evil-doer. Fiercely destructive and cloaked in flames, the hellhound will hunt down your enemies and fetch their heads to play with. Good boy.

creepy crawlies Snakes, and spiders, and centipedes, oh my! These ghastly critters can be a villain's delight, provided you are not too squeamish. They're quiet company, but you can snack on them when they multiply.

*The fuffy white cat and the hellhound
are favored pets of evil-doers.*

Entertaining at home is an excellent way to increase your social status.

Entertaining

Villains who make a heap of friends may want to consider inviting them over from time to time. Entertaining at home is an excellent way to increase your social status. It's also a convenient time to bump off any potential rivals or evil-doers who've stuck you with the dinner check. Party on!

party preparation   Planning a successful party is a complicated endeavor. Preparation is key, and there are many questions you must ask yourself: What kind of music? Do you want dancing? Games? Looting?

Choose your guests carefully. Aliens and demons tend not to get along, and it's always awkward when mad scientists fight with their creations. Prevent such ugly events by inviting only the coolest evil-doers to your party, unless you count on fights as part of the entertainment.

Your lair will need to be spruced up. Let the dragon out, and try to spend at least ten minutes cleaning. Decorate with the usual spiders and skeletons. If you're feeling fancy, you might want to embellish with a caged slime monster or some streamers. Put out some tasty refreshments, and when the sky finally darkens, open your doors and wait for your guests to arrive.

Keep in mind that many of your visitors will be "fashionably late." That's all right—they'll show up once they're done invading whatever country they're after that day. When they finally arrive, greet them warmly, and point them toward the poisonous punch.

Top Evil Party Themes

under the sea It's an aquatic adventure as creatures from the deep rise up and party with your pals! Tentacled bartenders, underwater cities, and motion sickness are just a few of the elements you'll enjoy with this great choice.

fall of Rome Enjoy every decadence and some catchy fiddle music as Rome burns to the ground. Don your toga, drink and eat to your heart's content, and don't forget to use the vomitorium when you're through.

nightmare realm All your guests' worst fears are realized at this party where nightmares come true! Up With People, the lambada, and a no-host bar—your guests won't be able to stop screaming!

totally tiki The island natives are restless, and boy do they like to party! Get ready to worship pagan gods and throw virgins into a volcano in this tiki-themed paradise sure to enthrall your grass-skirted guests.

space invaders The aliens have arrived, and they're hungry for humans! That doesn't mean they don't like to party, though, so put on a space suit and prepare to dance the night away as your space brethren try to convince you that *To Serve Man* is not a cookbook.

pajama party Grab a sleeping bag and a toothbrush because you're staying over tonight in your best friend's lair! Play secret kissing games, do each other's hair, and cast terrible hexes at this classic all-night party. Light as a feather, stiff as a board.

end of the world The apocalypse is here, so it's time to party like never before! Watch the seas boil and the sky fall as fire consumes the earth and leaves humanity nothing but a memory. There's still time for a quick drink, though, so grab them while they're cold!

Totally Tiki.

Pajama Party.

good party tricks Sometimes it's hard to get your party rolling. Your guests stay off the dance floor no matter how hypnotic the beat, and even the Chex Mix fails to bring a smile. To counteract this lethargy you need drastic measures. It's time for party tricks.

Villains not yet versed in the occult should learn to perform magic to enhance their usual dirty tricks. Classics like "Make the Hero Disappear" and "Saw the Sidekick in Half" are great crowd-pleasers, and you'll get even bigger laughs when you claim you can't put the sidekick back together. When you finish by transforming yourself into an armor-plated robotic juggernaut, you'll get a standing ovation!

While they may seem juvenile, balloon animals are another great way to get cheers. No one can resist balloon scorpions, worms, toads, or bloated ticks. If you really want to impress your guests, wow them with your amazing ability to read minds. Embarass the hell out of them.

While they may seem juvenile, balloon animals are another great way to get cheers.

dance for evil-doers   For your party to be a real success, there will have to be dancing. Even demons like to kick up their heels now and then, and, as such nefarious characters as the Lord of the Dance have shown us, it can be a fiendish thing indeed.

First you'll want to choose the music. It can be acid rock, techno, or even the weeping of your prisoners, as long as there's a beat you can dance to. Ghost bands are fun, although they'll probably only know the oldies. Artificially intelligent robot DJs are cheap but unpredictable. Another fun option: reanimated mariachis. Olé!

Next, you'll need a dance floor. Clear away your failed experiments and piles of spell books. Keep in mind that guests with tentacles may need extra room to really flail about. Black lights, strobes, night-vision goggles, spinning disco balls, interdimensional gateways, and wormholes will guarantee a trippy dance party.

All that's left is to get your fellow villains out on the dance floor. This may take some doing, as Necromancers and Galactic Tyrants tend to be a bit self-conscious about their bodies. But even the most hardened henchman can't resist the evil of Ricky Martin. Put on "La Vida Loca," and you'll soon have all the bad boys dancing like crazy!

Black lights, strobes, night-vision goggles, spinning disco balls, interdimensional gateways, and wormholes will guarantee a trippy dance party.

quick party recipes Your guests are likely to be hungry from a long day of looting and pillaging, so you'd best prepare some dishes to quell their monstrous appetites.

When it comes to hors d'oeuvres, the more fetid, the better.

finger foods

Human fingers
Saltine crackers
Cheese
Garnish

These are quite easy. Simply place the fingers on saltines and stick pieces of cheese between them. Add a bit of garnish, and you've got a tasty treat that can't be beat!

shish kebabs

One pixie or wood sprite
Fresh vegetables
Barbeque sauce

Chop the pixie into approximately eight pieces, and then place the bits between vegetables on a shish kebab skewer. Douse in barbecue sauce, grill over a fire for ten minutes, and enjoy!

cocktails

1 ounce gin
1 ounce brandy
1 ounce type O blood
Splash of lemon juice

Find a mixing glass and fill it to the brim with ice. Pour in gin, brandy, and blood, and then shake thoroughly until properly mixed. Add lemon juice, and your guests won't be able to get enough of this delicious drink!

Scheduling

evil day planner   Many villains suffer from an inability to keep their lives in order. Appointments are forgotten, dinner dates put off, masquerade balls left unattended. It's hard to conquer the world and still have a life, so it is highly suggested you obtain a day planner. With one of these withered books by your side, you'll be able to keep your social calendar full and nary forget an evil deed again!

MONDAY

8:00 AM · Weekly meeting with minions

11:00 AM · Call realtor

Noon · Lunch at cemetery

4:00 PM · Dentist appt.

6:00 PM · Paintball!

TUESDAY

9:00 AM · Restock poison supply

Noon · Therapy appt.

2:00 PM · Photocopy taxes

3:00 PM · Free Ebola monkey from cage

5:00 PM · "Grocery" shopping

WEDNESDAY

9:00 AM · Pick up dry cleaning

3:00 PM · Drop mom off at senior center

5:00 PM · Drain moat

6:00 PM · Start the BBQ

8:00 PM · Dinner with Dark Lord

THURSDAY

10:00 AM · Overthrow peace process

2:00 PM · Get tires rotated

4:00 PM · Attend "Building a Better You" seminar

9:00 PM · Create life in basement

FRIDAY

8:00 AM · Monthly report due

10:00 AM · Call Bob re: lawnmower

3:00 PM · Replace boss with pod person

5:00 PM · Buy lottery ticket!!!

8:00 PM · Disco dance party

SATURDAY

8:00 AM · Step aerobics with Vicky

10:00 AM · Clean dungeon

2:00 PM · Pay bills

3:00 PM · Reorganize record collection

Midnight · Unspeakable ritual of spooky doom

SUNDAY

10:00 AM · Visit Aunt Nancy (pick up mail)

Noon · Do Laundry

3:00 PM · Beach volleyball tournament

5:00 PM · Twirl mustache

8:00 PM · TV time— America's Funniest Home Videos!

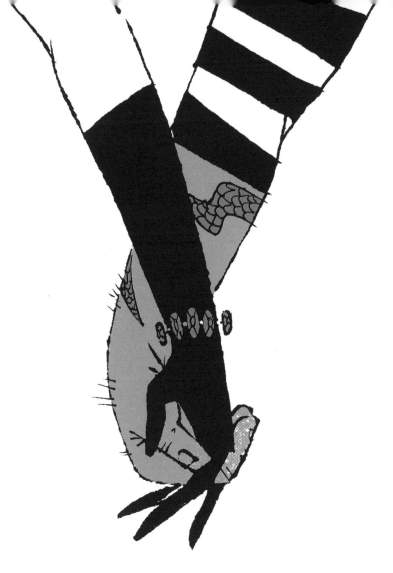

*Many villains and villainesses lack the necessary
social niceties to find romance.*

Dating

Every Warlord needs his Vice-Partner, and every Sorceress Queen needs her Prince Consort. Sadly, however, many villains and villainesses lack the necessary social niceties to find romance. They don't know what wilted flowers to send or what sweet nothings to hiss, and so spend their lives alone and bitter. For you, however, that's all about to change.

how to get a date   Walk an interesting pet creature at the dog park or go to the local hideout and look around. Could any fiends you encounter be a future spouse? There's only one way to find out!

This is the point at which many evil-doers experience jitters. You can defy all that is good and right without breaking a sweat, but as soon as you get a whiff of the right pheromones you turn to jelly. Well, buck up. Here are a few opening lines that should help:

"Is it infernally hot in here, or is it just you?"

"Your eyes are like two lurid pools of oil-slicked water!"

"What a gruesome furry beast you've got on that leash!"

"I really like your costume (jumpsuit, tail, pointy fingernails, sharpened teeth, fright wig, neck bolts, whatever)!"

"That cat-o-nine-tails would look perfect on my dungeon floor."

"Want to blow up the world together?"

Compliment their looks, brains, vehicle, army of trained spiders, or other pets, and then take a deep breath and ask your love-prey out. The worst that can happen is rejection, or being turned to stone.

looking your best   So you've got a date with the sorceress down the block, and you think you're ready to go. Hold on a moment . . . You're not going out like that, are you?

You'll want to start by choosing an outfit. We suggest wearing all jet black or blood red, although tombstone gray will work if you're a winter. Don't go casual—you want to make a wicked impression here. As for accessories, chains are always a nice touch, as are evil amulets and charms. Avoid anything with jagged spikes until you know each other better, as they may impale your date and bring the night to a quick end.

Grooming should be next on your list. What hairstyle suits you best—oily, stringy, or snakes? All are fine choices. Need to remove any tattoos that have lost their pizzazz? Do so without pause.

Dental hygiene is also very important, so be sure to brush those fangs! Back and forth, left and right, and then back and forth again. You will also want to pay attention to any claws and horns, as they tend to attract grime and mildew.

On a side note, it is probably not wise to trust any magic mirrors you might possess. They have a tendency to claim that you are the fairest of them all, but we all know they're suck-ups and outright liars. Trust your own instincts.

You'll want to start by choosing an outfit.

*On the first date you will make your impression and determine
the possibility of any future relationship.*

the first date   The time has come for your first date. This may seem like a terrifying endeavor, for it is here you will make your first impression and determine the possibility of any future relationship. But there's no need to get hysterical, so put down that noose and get ready to make this a night you won't forget.

Start by meeting your date and heading somewhere romantic. A popular eatery is best. Engage him or her or it in conversation, talking about any villages you've recently conquered or dead bodies you've managed to successfully reanimate. A quick joke is also recommended to break the tension. Try the one about the happy pixie and the exceptionally large mallet.

When it's time to order dinner, suggest a lovely toad stew or scorpions sautéed in a blood sauce. Engage in conversation, and try to show interest. Ask about work, family, what schooling he or she or it has in the black arts. If at any point you have to go to the bathroom, excuse yourself quietly and make sure your hair/face/pseudopods haven't smudged.

After dinner take in a show—mayhap a supernatural comedy, or a nice, light slasher flick. As an alternative you can always go to an all-night cybercafé and wreak havoc together. Your date will laugh and cheer, and as the night nears its end you'll know you've made a devilishly good impression.

It's now time for the final part of the evening: the good-night kiss. Don't be scared. Give it all you've got and let him or her or it know how much you've enjoyed his or her or its company. Who knows? If you're lucky, you might be invited in for a sordid night of passion. (Warning: Dates with giant praying mantises tend to end with your head being bitten off, so watch yourself.)

keeping the romance alive After you've been dating a villain or villainess for a while, you may notice that the romance starts to wane. It's just not the same as it was before. Your Ice Queen doesn't seem as interested in oppressing the masses or casting arcane spells. Your ogre doesn't relish your Englishman flambé like he used to. Don't despair. The misanthropy and bad taste that once bound you two together can be revived with a jolt of imagination. You need to make an effort or you may lose your significant other completely.

Gifts are an excellent way to sweeten a fading toxic relationship. Nothing says "I adore you" like a still-beating heart, or that cursed idol you discovered on your last trip to Lemuria. Choose something long-lasting, such as a new depleted-uranium drawing-and-quartering set, or maybe an antique iron maiden.

Trips to exotic lands are another possibility. Transylvania is always a popular getaway, especially if you prefer mountainous border regions where you two can rub shoulders with blood-suckers. The lost continent of Atlantis is fun for snorkeling, or if you've grown gills, and it's still full of loot for tomb robbers. If you're low on cash you can opt for a romantic weekend instead, staying at the local haunted bed-and-breakfast or Gothic cemetery. The Travel section of this book offers more details if this is the path you choose.

Grand gestures, however, are probably your best bet. There's little that will cause a heart to swoon more than discovering that someone has taken over the world for you.

Nothing says "I adore you" like a still-beating heart.

To ease the pain of rejection, turn your former love into a toad.

methods for dealing with rejection   Sad to say, sometimes the person you love loves you not. Your main squeeze goes for someone with more suckers or bigger tentacles, or she dumps you for a usurping despot. She just can't see past the horns to the real you, preferring a fish-man instead. Well, it's time to grab a moldy handkerchief and wipe away those crocodile tears, because there are a few things you can do to ease away the humiliation:

🐚 Turn your former love into a toad.

🐚 Lock yourself in a tower of despair for several years and learn to play the violin.

🐚 Have your henchmen cheer you up with a catchy song-and-dance routine.

🐚 Crack all the mirrors in your house so your self-image improves.

🐚 Unleash your armies of destruction upon the world.

🐚 Write lots of Goth poetry and self-publish.

6

Travel

— ☠ —

Feeling a bit run down lately? It's probably because you haven't taken a vacation in eons! Even the most vigorous villain needs a break now and then, and a trip to someplace new does wonders for the soul (or empty pit, where it used to reside). Set some time aside, check the travel brochures, and get ready to enjoy an evil vacation. Go ahead—get lost.

Your Dream (or Nightmare) Vacation

packing for the trip The amount of luggage you will need depends upon your length of stay. If it's going to be just a few days, you can probably survive on one bag. Any longer, however, and you'll want one coffin for clothes and one for supplies, plus a magic expanding portmanteau to hold all your souvenirs. Be sure to pack the following:

clothing Don't hesitate to bring your best duds, be they wizard's robes, a straightjacket, or black spiked battle armor. Swimwear and flippers are also recommended.

identification You'll need your various passports to get through customs, but if you're on the run just bring your invisibility juice.

camera So you can relive meeting your favorite dictator or the King of the Zombies.

toiletries Your vacation won't be much fun if you don't have a way to maintain your claws and fangs.

sunscreen Essential if you are undead, or if you have not seen the light of day in fifty years.

spellbook Always good for a little light reading. Try out some new curses on the locals!

rooms and lodging Comfortable lodging with plenty of privacy is the key to a successful vacation. Time and time again villains just take the first hotel available, not realizing they've chosen a fleabag or, horror of horrors, a bed-and-breakfast. You'll want to examine your options beforehand, using the phone book, the Internet, and any flying monkeys at your disposal to determine your potential stay's quality.

Once you find a place that fits your needs, you will have to consider the price. Even if you can't afford it, there is no reason you can't stay at a four-skull hotel. You'll just need to barter with the management, pointing out the leaks, the smells, and the fact that you have a very large battle-ax in your hand.

It should be noted that all of this is moot if you don't bother to make a reservation first. You never know when the galactic warlords conference is coming into town, so be sure to contact the hotel well in advance.

Horror of horrors, a bed-and-breakfast.

avoiding tourist traps   Something to keep in mind as you travel the spooky world is that not every tourist spot is genuine. There are quite a few scams out there, nefarious outfits that trick villains into paying hard-earned funny money to see the largest werewolf in the Midwest when it's really just a hairy man in a mullet.

The best way to prevent such debacles is to investigate tourist sites before you go. See what previous visitors have to say about the Most Gangrenous Mummy Wraps in Minnesota. Was the tomb rot authentic? Did they leave feeling genuinely cursed? Do your homework.

Should you follow this advice and still run across a tourist trap, the entire day needn't be ruined. You can still enjoy it "ironically," as the hipsters do. Point and laugh and the loser tourists will think it's all real. Pose for cheesy photos with your face grinning through a hole. Buy a "My dad went to the haunted tar pits and all I got was this lousy T-shirt" T-shirt and you'll laugh and hiss about your misadventure for years to come.

going through customs   When traveling between countries you will have the inevitable problem of dealing with customs agents. You can't simply enter a foreign power with a lethal man-eating plant—that thing might have fruit flies. Customs is certainly a hassle, but there are some things you can do to make the experience easier.

- Travel under the name of someone less likely to be hassled, like the pope.

- Learn ahead of time which doomsday devices are prohibited on the flight.

- Pay a special fee to bring your robotic gorilla on board.

- Send any questionable objects via winged demon instead.

- Bribe troublesome custom officials with desirable items in your luggage—painkillers, contraband endangered species, dragon bone aphrodisiacs.

- Shout, "What's that?" and make a run for it.

- Drink your invisibility potion and simply walk through the line.

what to do if you lose your luggage   It's a situation every evil-doer fears: You're vacationing in another dimension when some foul miscreant distracts you and steals your luggage. It's a terrible misfortune, but it doesn't have to end with your lifelong slavery as a dishwasher.

First, you'll need to call home immediately. Instruct your henchmen to send a replacement coffin, change of clothes, chest of gold, toothbrush, and so on. You will then need to obtain some cash for the interim, so try regaling the locals with tales of your supreme might before begging them for quarters. If that fails, break-dance. You should earn enough to get by until your luggage arrives.

Bear in mind that you can prepare for such occurrences by taking security precautions ahead of time. Lock your suitcase tight, and booby-trap it with pepper spray and slime. You can also train "alligator" luggage to devour anyone who opens it without authorization. You may lose your bags, but the thief will lose limbs.

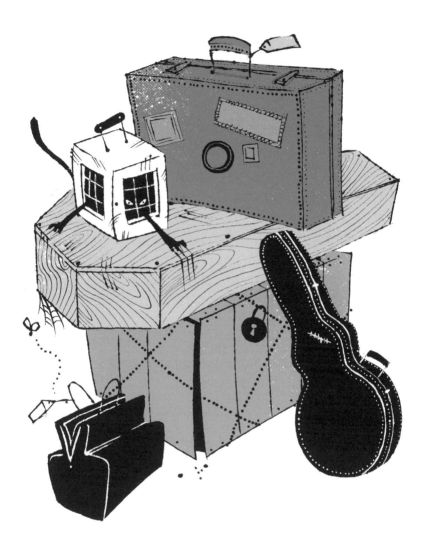

Losing your luggage: It's a terrible misfortune, but it doesn't have to end with your lifelong slavery as a dishwasher.

Destinations

dark castles   Some of the most popular destinations for villains are dark castles and impregnable fortresses. These towers of unending sorrow provide nothing but horror for the locals—what a wonderful spot to hang your hat for a bit! They house all manner of musty rooms and secret passages, and their armies of destruction can usually be rented for a modest fee. You can also often find old ghosts within who will gladly tell their tales of betrayal, and whose spinning-head tricks are sure to entertain the kids, if this is a family vacation. Put this unholy spot on your itinerary today!

spooky forests   You may want to consider visiting the forests of the wild while on your vacation. Deep woods are traditional for dark rituals (that's why competing villains posing as self-righteous timber barons want to turn forests into coffin planks). Headless horsemen can be conjured up to provide ample atmosphere. Frightening campers is a great diversion, and any will-o'-the-wisps are sure to provoke interesting conversation. Many forests even contain gingerbread houses, a tasty source of food and good place to drop off the kids for the day.

universities   For nostalgia's sake, why not stop by your alma mater? You can sit in on a class of Necromancy 101, join the hazing of criminal masterminds, mentor undergrads to sell their souls to the military-industrial machine, and attend a keg party of the local mad-scientist fraternity. This is also an excellent opportunity to put on the black and blue again, cheering for the Screaming Vultures as you pelt the opposing team with rotten eggs. Go, team!

Towers of unending sorrow are a wonderful spot to hang your hat for a bit!

10:00am-4:00pm

tombs You'll also be sure to want to check out any local grave-yards while on vacation. You can take a nap in one of the more luxurious coffins, or dig up an old friend to chat awhile. Just remember to respect the local undead, as those zombies and ghouls were here before you and you're traipsing on their turf. In faraway lands there's nothing quite like appreciating the architecture of ancient tombs, and dodging the slicing blades and pit traps that come with the territory.

dark monuments Don't forget that most tourist towns have a number of interesting monuments to visit during your stay— perhaps a large statue with a pigeon on its head celebrating a villain's triumph, plaques marking the location where a ravenous demon was summoned, or tremendous houses of misery and pain. You can also opt for the more personal route and visit the old withered tree dedicated in honor of your mentor. Give that nefarious fiend the proper respect, and then cackle with glee knowing that one day you'll have a bigger monument than them all.

alternate dimensions For a truly exotic vacation, consider taking your family to an alternate dimension. Accessible through the space-time vortex and dark rituals, these nightmarish vistas bring a new definition to the word *weird*. You'll spend your days avoiding monstrous aliens and unexpected showers of frogs, and your nights swimming through lakes of tapioca muck. The rules of reality don't apply here, so be prepared for M. C. Escher–like landscapes and long negotiations with the king of the potato people. Exceptionally bizarre, it's a mind-bending experience the little ones won't soon forget.

*Alternate dimensions are a mind-bending experience
the little ones won't soon forget.*

Afterword

By now, your life should have changed completely. Your lair should be a horrific masterpiece that inspires terror in your fellow man. Your job should be strangely tolerable and a recruiting ground for the hordes who would follow you. Your nights should be filled with screams, spent with a beautiful succubus (or a hairy gargoyle), or whatever you like.

Don't thank anyone but yourself! You possessed the ambition and vision necessary to bring about these improvements, to change from casual evil-doer to jet-setting villain of doom! Congratulations! Hold your multiple heads high, and go forth and conquer! If you're not already on the evening news, you will be soon!

Voila!